# The Drug War in Mexico
## Confronting a Shared Threat

D1132312

COUNCIL *on*
FOREIGN
RELATIONS

*Center for Preventive Action*

Council Special Report No. 60
March 2011

David A. Shirk

# The Drug War in Mexico
## Confronting a Shared Threat

The Council on Foreign Relations (CFR) is an independent, nonpartisan membership organization, think tank, and publisher dedicated to being a resource for its members, government officials, business executives, journalists, educators and students, civic and religious leaders, and other interested citizens in order to help them better understand the world and the foreign policy choices facing the United States and other countries. Founded in 1921, CFR carries out its mission by maintaining a diverse membership, with special programs to promote interest and develop expertise in the next generation of foreign policy leaders; convening meetings at its headquarters in New York and in Washington, DC, and other cities where senior government officials, members of Congress, global leaders, and prominent thinkers come together with Council members to discuss and debate major international issues; supporting a Studies Program that fosters independent research, enabling CFR scholars to produce articles, reports, and books and hold roundtables that analyze foreign policy issues and make concrete policy recommendations; publishing *Foreign Affairs*, the preeminent journal on international affairs and U.S. foreign policy; sponsoring Independent Task Forces that produce reports with both findings and policy prescriptions on the most important foreign policy topics; and providing up-to-date information and analysis about world events and American foreign policy on its website, CFR.org.

The Council on Foreign Relations takes no institutional positions on policy issues and has no affiliation with the U.S. government. All statements of fact and expressions of opinion contained in its publications are the sole responsibility of the author or authors.

Council Special Reports (CSRs) are concise policy briefs, produced to provide a rapid response to a developing crisis or contribute to the public's understanding of current policy dilemmas. CSRs are written by individual authors—who may be CFR fellows or acknowledged experts from outside the institution—in consultation with an advisory committee, and are intended to take sixty days from inception to publication. The committee serves as a sounding board and provides feedback on a draft report. It usually meets twice— once before a draft is written and once again when there is a draft for review; however, advisory committee members, unlike Task Force members, are not asked to sign off on the report or to otherwise endorse it. Once published, CSRs are posted on www.cfr.org.

For further information about CFR or this Special Report, please write to the Council on Foreign Relations, 58 East 68th Street, New York, NY 10065, or call the Communications office at 212.434.9888. Visit our website, CFR.org.

To submit a letter in response to a Council Special Report for publication on our website, CFR.org, you may send an email to CSReditor@cfr.org. Alternatively, letters may be mailed to us at: Publications Department, Council on Foreign Relations, 58 East 68th Street, New York, NY 10065. Letters should include the writer's name, postal address, and daytime phone number. Letters may be edited for length and clarity, and may be published online. Please do not send attachments. All letters become the property of the Council on Foreign Relations and will not be returned. We regret that, owing to the volume of correspondence, we cannot respond to every letter.

This report is printed on paper that is certified by SmartWood to the standards of the Forest Stewardship Council, which promotes environmentally responsible, socially beneficial, and economically viable management of the world's forests.

**Mixed Sources**
Product group from well-managed forests and other controlled sources
www.fsc.org   Cert no. SW-COC-001530
© 1996 Forest Stewardship Council
FSC

# Contents

# Foreword

Since the 1970s, the cross-border trade in drugs and guns has brought both immense profits and terrible destruction to the United States and Mexico. Some estimates place the annual profits of Mexico's drug trade at 3 percent to 4 percent of the country's GDP—on the order of $30 billion per year—and around half a million people are said to earn a substantial portion of their income through the narcotics business. The business, however, is not without its risks and costs. Since Mexico's president, Felipe Calderón, effectively declared war on the drug cartels in 2006, more than thirty-five thousand people have died in drug-related violence in Mexico.

Nor is the United States immune from the effects of the drug trade. The ruthlessness of drug trafficking organizations is already well known in this country, particularly, though not exclusively, in the inner cities, and the violence of Mexico's drug war is now beginning to spill over the border. Border patrols are already costing the country more than $3 billion per year and obstructing billions more in legitimate trade. Yet the United States is hardly an innocent victim. Nearly half of adult Americans admit to having tried drugs in the past, and the United States remains the world's largest consumer of illegal drugs. It is also the world's largest supplier of weapons, which fuel the drug war in a more direct way. Fully 10 percent of America's gun dealers line the Mexican border, and the country's permissive gun laws make it an inexpensive and convenient source of powerful guns, ammunition, and explosives. Speaking after his recent summit with President Calderón, U.S. president Barack Obama acknowledged this reality. "We are very mindful," he said, "that the battle President Calderón is fighting inside of Mexico is not just his battle; it's also ours. We have to take responsibility just as he's taking responsibility."

In this Council Special Report, David A. Shirk, director of the Trans-Border Institute at the University of San Diego, analyzes the steps that the United States and Mexico can take to more effectively combat drug violence. Though Calderón's military-led effort has splintered the major drug cartels, it has not diminished their strength—or political influence—sufficiently to prosecute them in the courts rather than in the streets. Nor is Mexico's criminal justice system robust enough to pose a real challenge to cartel leaders. It remains seriously underfunded, riddled with corruption, and deeply mistrusted by the public. And while American efforts to support the military and shore up the justice system have been substantial, efforts to address the economic and social conditions that encourage people to join the drug trade are, as yet, insufficient.

To address these challenges, the author outlines a series of recommendations. In addition to improving cooperation between U.S., Mexican, and Central American security authorities, he writes, the United States must expand its aid to nonmilitary fronts in the long-running war on drugs. Washington should, he argues, assist Mexico's criminal justice system as it pursues a wide-ranging set of organizational, operational, and cultural reforms to improve its effectiveness, efficiency, and professionalism. Moreover, the United States should increase funding for job creation, microfinance, and other economic aid to expand opportunities outside the drug trade. Finally, he recommends that the United States explore alternatives to its current drug laws; while legalization may not be the answer, he says, focusing exclusively on punishing suppliers and users has not proven a successful strategy.

*The Drug War in Mexico: Confronting a Shared Threat* thus provides a fresh look at one of the most important security threats in the Western Hemisphere and suggests recommendations for policy in both Washington and Mexico City. There can be little doubt that the social, economic, and political challenges posed by drug trafficking are grave for both countries. Purposeful and immediate action is warranted, and this report provides thoughtful and thought-provoking guidance for those looking to begin.

**Richard N. Haass**
*President*
Council on Foreign Relations
March 2011

# Acknowledgments

I would like to thank the Council on Foreign Relations (CFR) for the opportunity to author this Council Special Report, and for bringing attention to the complexities of Mexico's current security crisis at such a critical juncture in the U.S.-Mexico relationship. I am especially grateful to CFR President Richard N. Haass, Director of Studies and Maurice R. Greenberg Chair James M. Lindsay, Center for Preventive Action (CPA) Director Paul Stares, and CPA Fellow Micah Zenko for their careful reading and comments on multiple drafts of this report.

My analysis benefited from discerning comments, corrections, and suggestions from a distinguished advisory committee of leading experts on U.S.-Mexico affairs, whose members are identified at the end of this report. Professor Peter H. Smith, who chaired this advisory committee and read several drafts of the report with characteristic gusto, has been an influential mentor for many years and I am privileged to have worked so closely with him on this effort. John Bailey of Georgetown University also played a critical role in the development of the report.

Numerous U.S. and Mexican government officials generously shared their time and insights, for which I am extremely grateful. Moreover, several colleagues provided invaluable input as I wrote the report, which also benefited from the steadfast research assistance and support of Morayma Jimenez, Nicole Ramos, and Elisse Larouche. I am also deeply indebted to my colleagues at the Trans-Border Institute: Stephanie Borrowdale, Anna Cearley, Theresa Firestine, Cory Molzahn, Charles Pope, Viridiana Ríos, and Octavio Rodriguez.

Working on this report gave me a hearty appreciation for the fine work of CFR Publications editors Patricia Dorff and Lia Norton, as well as Lisa Shields and Sarah Doolin from the Communications team. It was extremely rewarding to work with CPA's exceptional staff, including Rebecca R. Friedman and my former student Elise Vaughan. Last, but not least, my work on this project could not have happened without the blessing of having a patient wife and a well-behaved child.

I learned so much from this process and from the many contributors noted. I thank them all while fully acknowledging my own responsibility for any errors, omissions, or flawed assertions in this report.

This publication was made possible by a grant from the Carnegie Corporation of New York. The statements made and views expressed herein are solely my own.

**David A. Shirk**

# Acronyms

| | |
|---|---|
| ABA | American Bar Association |
| ATF | Department of Justice Bureau of Alcohol, Tobacco, Firearms, and Explosives |
| BLM | border liaison mechanism |
| CALEA | Commission on Accreditation for Law Enforcement Agencies |
| CARICOM | Caribbean Community and Common Market |
| CARSI | Central America Regional Security Initiative |
| CBSI | Caribbean Basin Security Initiative |
| C-TPAT | Customs-Trade Partnership Against Terrorism |
| DEA | Drug Enforcement Administration |
| DOD | Department of Defense |
| DTO | drug trafficking organization |
| FBI | Federal Bureau of Investigation |
| FDIC | Federal Deposit Insurance Corporation |
| GATT | General Agreement on Tariffs and Trade |
| INL | Bureau of International Narcotics Affairs and Law Enforcement |
| NAFTA | North American Free Trade Agreement |
| NCSC | National Center for State Courts |
| NORTHCOM | U.S. Northern Command |
| NSC | National Security Council |
| PAN | National Action Party |
| PRI | Institutional Revolutionary Party |

| | |
|---|---|
| SEC | U.S. Securities and Exchange Commission |
| SENTRI | Secure Electronic Network for Travelers Rapid Inspection |
| USAID | United States Agency for International Development |
| WHA | Bureau of Western Hemisphere Affairs |

*Council Special Report*

# Introduction

Mexico is in the midst of a worsening security crisis. Explosive clashes and territorial disputes among powerful drug trafficking organizations (DTOs) have killed more than thirty-five thousand people since President Felipe Calderón took office in December 2006. The geography of that violence is limited but continues to spread, and its targets include a growing number of government officials, police officers, journalists, and individuals unrelated to the drug trade. The Mexican government has made the war on drugs its top priority and has even called in the military to support the country's weak police and judicial institutions. Even so, few Mexican citizens feel safer today than they did ten years ago, and most believe that their government is losing the fight.

Despite the most dismal assessments, the Mexican state has not failed, nor has it confronted a growing insurgent movement.[1] Moreover, violence elsewhere in the Western Hemisphere is far worse than in Mexico. Whereas 45,000 homicides (14 per 100,000) have occurred in Mexico since 2007, Brazil and Colombia saw more than 80,000 (20 per 100,000) and 50,000 (30 per 100,000) murders, respectively.[2] Even so, the country's violent organized crime groups represent a real and present danger to Mexico, the United States, and neighboring countries. The tactics they use often resemble those of terrorists and insurgents, even though their objectives are profit seeking rather than politically motivated. Meanwhile, although the Mexican state retains democratic legitimacy and a firm grasp on the overwhelming majority of Mexican territory, some DTOs capitalize on antigovernment sentiments and have operational control of certain limited geographic areas. DTOs have also corrupted officials at all levels of government, and they increasingly lash out against Mexican government officials and ordinary citizens. The February 2011 killing of a U.S. immigration and customs agent signals that U.S. law enforcement officials are now in the crosshairs. If current security trends continue to worsen, the emergence of a genuine insurgent movement, the proliferation of "ungoverned spaces," and the deliberate and sustained targeting of U.S. government personnel will become more likely.

The United States has much to gain by helping strengthen its southern neighbor and even more to lose if it does not. The cumulative effects of an embattled Mexican state harm the United States and a further reduction of Mexican state capacity is both unacceptable and a clear motivation for U.S. preventive action.

First, the weaker the Mexican state, the greater difficulty the United States will have in controlling the nearly two-thousand-mile border. Spillover violence, in which DTOs bring their fight to U.S. soil, is a remote worst-case scenario.[3] Even so, lawlessness south of the border directly affects the United States. A weak Mexican government increases the flow of both illegal immigrants and contraband (such as drugs, money, and weapons) into the United States. As the dominant wholesale distributors of illegal drugs to U.S. consumers, Mexican traffickers are also the single greatest domestic organized crime threat within the United States, operating in every state and hundreds of cities, selling uncontrolled substances that directly endanger the health and safety of millions of ordinary citizens.

Second, economically, Mexico is an important market for the United States. As a member of the North American Free Trade Agreement (NAFTA), it is one of only seventeen states with which the United States has a free trade pact, outside the General Agreement on Tariffs and Trade (GATT). The United States has placed nearly $100 billion of foreign direct investment in Mexico. Mexico is also the United States' third-largest trade partner, the third-largest source of U.S. imports, and the second-largest exporter of U.S. goods and services—with potential for further market growth as the country develops. Trade with Mexico benefits the U.S. economy, and the market collapse that would likely accompany a deteriorated security situation could hamper U.S. economic recovery.

Third, Mexican stability serves as an important anchor for the region. With networks stretching into Central America, the Caribbean, and the Andean countries, Mexican DTOs undermine the security and reliability of other U.S. partners in the hemisphere, corrupting high-level officials, military operatives, and law enforcement personnel; undermining due process and human rights; reducing public support for counter-drug efforts; and even provoking hostility toward the United States. Given the fragility of some Central American and Caribbean states, expansion of DTO operations and violence into the region would have a gravely destabilizing effect.

Fourth, the unchecked power and violence of these Mexican DTOs present a substantial humanitarian concern and have contributed to forced migration and numerous U.S. asylum requests. If the situation were to worsen, a humanitarian emergency might lead to an unmanageable flow of people into the United States. It would also adversely affect the many U.S. citizens living in Mexico.

Solving the crisis is not only in the U.S. national interest but also in part a U.S. responsibility, given that U.S. drug consumption, firearms, and cash have fueled much of Mexico's recent violence.[4] The United States should therefore take full advantage of the unprecedented resolve of Mexican authorities to work bilaterally to address a common threat. The best hope for near-term progress is to bolster U.S. domestic law enforcement efforts to curb illicit drug distribution, firearms smuggling, and money laundering. In the intermediate term, the United States should also both make an overall commitment to preventing and treating drug abuse and other societal ills caused by drugs and reevaluate the effectiveness of current U.S. and international drug policies. Additionally, with an eye to strengthening Mexico in the longer term, the United States should redouble rule of law and economic assistance to Mexico, with an emphasis on professionalizing the judicial sector and creating economic alternatives to a life of crime. To prevent Mexico's problems from spreading to Central America and the Caribbean, the United States should also work actively to reinvigorate and adapt regional security frameworks for the transnational challenges of the post–Cold War era.

## A SHARED THREAT

On a day-to-day basis, no other country affects the United States as Mexico does. More than ever, Mexico and the United States are deeply interdependent: they are connected by more than $300 billion in annual cross-border trade, tens of millions of U.S. and Mexican citizens in binational families, and the everyday interactions of more than 14 million people living along the nearly two-thousand-mile shared border.

Unfortunately, U.S.-Mexico interdependence has also been marked by the proliferation of powerful transnational organized crime syndicates and extreme violence that has killed tens of thousands of Mexicans and hundreds of U.S. citizens in recent years. The ability of organized crime to corrupt elected officials and law enforcement authorities has long compromised U.S.-Mexico security cooperation, but now the Mexican government's increased reliance on the military raises new dangers of institutional corruption and human rights abuses. Moreover, growing public frustration has led to increased vigilantism and support for heavy-handed security measures that lack transparency and violate due process. All of these trends present grave challenges for Mexico and have already begun to spread to Central America.[5] Given the threat to U.S. interests and stability in the region, the United States, Mexico, and several Central American countries have already embarked on an unprecedented security partnership known as the Mérida Initiative, a three-year, nearly $1.4 billion aid package to provide U.S. equipment, training and technical assistance, counternarcotics intelligence sharing, and rule of law promotion programs in Mexico and Central America.[6] Despite these important efforts, the proliferation of violence and the relentless flow of drugs into the United States continue. Improving the U.S. response to this shared threat demands a clear understanding of Mexico's security crisis, counter-drug efforts in Mexico, and the role of the United States.

# Understanding Mexico's Security Crisis

Mexico's security crisis is complex and deeply rooted in the country's recent economic struggles and political development. Starting in the 1970s, economic fluctuations and uncertainty contributed to heightened unemployment, reduced labor market opportunities, and significant spikes in criminal activity. In the 1980s and 1990s, the introduction of free market reforms produced mixed results, and the gradual implementation of the reforms pushed many ordinary Mexicans to find alternative employment in an expanding underground economy that, by some estimates, accounted for 40 percent of all economic activity—including street vendors, pirate taxis, and a burgeoning market for ostensibly secondhand goods actually stolen from local sources (such as auto parts, electronics, and the like).[7]

As the global economy grew, so did a diversified and innovative network of illicit entrepreneurs, and drug trafficking presented the most lucrative black market opportunities. Increases in U.S. consumption of illicit psychotropic substances (especially cocaine) in the 1970s and tougher counter-drug efforts in Colombia and the Gulf of Mexico shifted drug production and trafficking routes to Mexico in the 1980s. Although Mexico had been a longtime source of marijuana, opium, and synthetic drugs for the U.S. market, its rise as a transit point for cocaine created profitable new employment opportunities for the estimated 450,000 people who rely on drug trafficking as a significant source of income today. Official estimates suggest that drug trafficking activities now account for 3 percent to 4 percent of Mexico's more than $1 trillion GDP.[8]

Mexico's domestic security situation began to deteriorate in the mid-1990s, largely due to a severe economic crisis, which brought sharp increases in robbery and property crime. Even after the economy stabilized, infighting among drug traffickers continued and the diversification of their illicit activities to include kidnappings, robberies, human smuggling, and extortion made DTO violence a major risk for ordinary Mexicans. The annual number of drug-related homicides has increased more than sixfold since 2005; in 2010 alone, the Mexican newspaper *Reforma* documented more than eleven thousand killings. All told, the Mexican government estimates that from January 2007 to late 2010, of perhaps forty-five thousand homicides (roughly twelve per hundred thousand people), more than thirty-two thousand were drug related.[9]

Although not apparent from the raw statistics, Mexican drug violence is highly concentrated. Two-thirds of drug-related homicides occur in just five of the thirty-two Mexican states and roughly 80 percent in just 168 of the 2,456 municipalities. The density of violence has made major trafficking cities like Ciudad Juárez and Culiacán among the deadliest places in the world. With just over one million inhabitants, Juárez had more than 2,700 homicides in 2010, more than the combined annual totals for New York (532), Chicago (435), Philadelphia (304), Los Angeles (297), Washington, DC (131), and Miami-Dade (84). Violence is increasingly directed toward the government. Dozens of elected officials, hundreds of police and military personnel, and intelligence agents working with U.S. law enforcement in the fight against organized crime have been murdered.[10] Also, the murders and disappearances of sixty-seven reporters over the past decade have sent a chilling message to the media—the eyes, ears, and voice of civil society—and have made Mexico one of the world's most dangerous places for journalists.[11]

The worsening of crime, violence, corruption, and dysfunctional criminal justice has overshadowed Mexico's democratic and economic advances. In 2000, Mexico celebrated a critical watershed, as democratic elections produced the country's first peaceful transfer of power between opposing political parties. Vicente Fox, a member of the country's oldest opposition party, the National Action Party (PAN), assumed the presidency after seventy-one years of uninterrupted rule by the Institutional Revolutionary Party (PRI). In consolidating its new democracy, Mexico has made impressive efforts to improve the transparency and credibility of elections, protect the rights of indigenous people, strengthen judicial independence, and even investigate past government abuses. Moreover, after decades of crisis and restructuring, Mexico's economy has shown remarkable stability and even modest progress in recent years, with gains in poverty reduction and the emergence of a middle class.

# Current Counter-Drug Efforts in Mexico

What stands out about Mexico's recent drug-related violence is the extent to which political change and counternarcotics efforts have actually intensified the competition among DTOs and the violent conflicts between them.

Eradication and interdiction efforts targeting the Mexican drug trade began more than fifty years ago, but for most of that period few serious efforts to dismantle major DTOs were made.[12] Indeed, well into the 1980s, many current top cartel operatives—virtually all of them with roots in Sinaloa—operated largely undisturbed within a loosely knit alliance that controlled different commissions, or *plazas*, for smuggling drugs into the United States and benefited from a highly permissive environment.[13] Mexico's centralized, single-party political system enabled DTOs to create a system-wide network of corruption that ensured distribution rights, market access, and even official government protection for drug traffickers in exchange for lucrative bribes.[14]

Mexican officials now want to break the major DTOs down into smaller pieces, transforming a national security threat to a public security problem. However, smaller does not necessarily mean more manageable. As organized crime groups have fractionalized and decentralized, the result has been a much more chaotic and unpredictable pattern of violent conflict. In the 1990s there were four major DTOs; today there are at least seven.

## MEXICO'S MILITARIZED RESPONSE

Greater militarization of the war on drugs has been a hallmark of the Calderón administration's approach. Escalating what has been a permanent campaign against drug trafficking, the federal government has since 2006 deployed tens of thousands of troops to man checkpoints, establish street patrols, shadow local police forces, and oversee other domestic law enforcement functions in high–drug violence states.[15]

However, even as a short-term measure, the effectiveness of Mexico's military strategy raises serious questions. First, it has brought unpredictable results and mixed success in reducing violence, sometimes only shifting it to different states.[16] Second, the military's role sometimes leads to confusion and confrontation among authorities, as in Baja California, where the head military commander issued damning accusations of corruption against state and local law enforcement authorities in 2008. Third, the militarization of public security in Mexico has contributed to greater military corruption and led to a sixfold increase from 2006 to 2009 in accusations of serious human rights abuses by members of the military. Finally, the high incidence of desertion among Mexican armed forces—averaging around twenty thousand troops per year—presents a considerable hazard.[17] Although most deserters are low-level, recently enlisted personnel, a worst-case illustration is the Zetas, a paramilitary enforcer group comprising elite former military forces recruited by the Gulf Cartel. Their defection from the Mexican military and subsequent break with the Gulf Cartel introduced new militarized tactics to the drug war, brought new forms of extreme violence (such as beheadings), and led other drug trafficking organizations to use similar methods.[18]

All of these trends threaten to erode the legitimacy of the military and the state itself in the eyes of the public. Nationally, support for the war on drugs is rapidly dwindling. Most Mexicans believe that the government is outmatched by the narco-traffickers, who enjoy at least some complicity, support, and even sympathy from other members of society.[19] Mexican government efforts—and U.S. support—could become tainted by a continued increase in alleged military abuses. In the long term, using Mexico's armed forces for law enforcement is unsustainable and the judicial sector eventually must reassume responsibility.

## REFORMING MEXICO'S JUDICIAL SECTOR

Mexico's security crisis is due not only to a lack of compliance with the law, but also to the failure of the government to enforce the law faithfully, effectively, and fairly. Effective rule of law is necessary to democratic governance. It requires a shift in the organizational models, operational strategies, and even the internal culture of police agencies and the judiciary to make each of these more responsive to the expectations of society, more accountable to the public, and more respectful of citizens' basic rights.[20]

Yet ten years after Mexico's first democratic transfer of power between opposing political parties, its police agencies continue to suffer from dangerous and deplorable working conditions, low professional standards, and severely limited resources. Police themselves believe that rampant corruption is institutionally predetermined and attributable to high-level infiltration by organized crime and inadequate internal investigations.[21] Their efforts to promote police reform have resulted in an alphabet soup of new and subsequently dismantled police agencies from the 1980s through the present. In another effort, the Calderón administration recently proposed dissolving municipal police forces and reintegrating them into state-level public security agencies, though what is really needed is greater professionalization and more checks and balances throughout the criminal justice system.[22]

Currently, because citizens have no confidence in Mexico's justice sector, an estimated three-quarters of crimes go unreported.[23] Moreover, because of institutional weaknesses, many reported cases are not investigated or witnesses to the crime fail to identify a suspect. The result is widespread criminal impunity, with perhaps one or two out of every hundred crimes resulting in a sentence.[24] Nevertheless, once a suspect has been identified, a guilty verdict is highly likely, in part because the use of torture, forced confessions, and poor investigative techniques often provide the basis for indictment and conviction.[25] Once in prison, inmates typically encounter horrendous conditions that encourage continued criminal behavior, frequent riots, and escapes.[26]

To address these problems, Mexican legislators passed a package of constitutional reforms in 2008. The legislation would radically alter the criminal justice system by introducing police and judicial reforms to strengthen public security, criminal investigations, due process protections for the accused, and efforts to combat organized crime.[27] If implemented, these reforms would help improve law enforcement, combat judicial sector corruption, and prevent systemic human rights abuses. At the current pace, however, the goal of implementing the reforms nationwide by 2016 is highly unlikely, and the upcoming 2012 presidential elections bring the fate of the reforms into question. Full implementation will require revising legal codes and procedures; physically modifying courtrooms, police investigative facilities, and jails for crime suspects; and retraining judges, court staffs, lawyers, and police. Moreover, the judicial reform initiative must overcome recent criticisms that it favors the interests of criminals over victims and constitutes an imperialist imposition of the U.S. legal system in Mexico.

To ensure support for the reform initiative, Mexican authorities will need to provide adequate professional training and public education programs to smooth the adjustment to this new system. Moreover, to monitor advances, make future adjustments, and ultimately win hearts and minds, authorities will need to develop performance indicators that can demonstrate the system's progress over time.

# The U.S. Role

As the world's largest consumer of drugs and its largest supplier of fire-arms, the United States is a direct contributor to Mexico's drug vio-lence. According to the 2009 National Survey on Drug Use and Health, roughly 8.7 percent of U.S. residents over the age of twelve—some 21.8 million people—had used drugs within the previous month.[28] Moreover, over the past three decades, a growing number of U.S. adults, including nearly half of individuals over the age of thirty-five, admit to some drug use during their lifetime. Because of the size of the U.S. black market for drugs and the inflationary effect of prohibition on prices, Mexican sup-pliers enjoy enormous gross revenues, estimated at $6 billion to $7 bil-lion annually, at least 70 percent coming from hard drugs like cocaine, heroin, methamphetamine, and other synthetics.[29] Although drug traf-fickers' financial operations are robust and sophisticated, and include the use of cyber technologies and offshore accounts, efforts to combat money-laundering operations have been weak. Mexico typically nets fewer than ten money-laundering convictions each year, and recent high-profile U.S. prosecutions targeting American Express, Bank of America, and Wells Fargo are more the exception than the rule.[30]

Firearms, ammunition, and explosives sold in the United States are also a major contributing factor to Mexico's violence. Mexican DTOs use a wide range of firearms, including some U.S.-manufactured hand grenades and rocket-propelled grenades, but the weapons of choice are AK-47- and AR-15-type rifles and high-caliber pistols. These are often imported legally to the United States from Europe, then sold illegally and in large numbers to surrogate or "straw" purchasers in the United States (with semiautomatic rifles frequently converted into select-fire machine guns). The United States is a convenient point of purchase for Mexican DTOs, given that an estimated 10 percent of U.S. gun deal-ers are located along the U.S.-Mexico border.[31] Moreover, there are few obstacles to the purchase of firearms, ammunition, and explosives, because powerful U.S. gun lobbies have effectively hamstrung efforts to enforce existing laws, combat firearms trafficking, or otherwise restrict access to deadly, high-powered weapons.[32] Failure to address money laundering and gun trafficking with greater commitment undermines Mexico's trust and may close the present window of opportunity for binational cooperation.

President Obama has pledged his support for international treaties that would facilitate information sharing, mutual legal assistance, and extradition to better combat arms trafficking, but these treaties have not yet been presented to the Senate for ratification.[33] At the same time, efforts to monitor gun trafficking, promote effective U.S. and Mexican law enforcement cooperation, and even enable collaboration among U.S. federal, state, and local agencies are constrained by a lack of access to aggregate trace data from the Department of Justice Bureau of Alcohol, Tobacco, Firearms, and Explosives (ATF) on guns linked to violent crimes. Still, some U.S. states have made progress in reducing gun trafficking and violence by adopting certain registration and permit requirements, gun possession laws, dealer inspection policies, criminal penalties, local ordinances, and reporting mechanisms for lost or stolen guns.[34] Ultimately, though, as with drugs, the illicit flow of firearms across the border will be difficult to control as long as market demand remains strong.

## OPPORTUNITIES FOR U.S.-MEXICO SECURITY COOPERATION

Security collaboration between the United States and Mexico has traditionally suffered from asymmetrical capabilities, divergent priorities, and frequent distrust. Even today, Mexicans tend to see their current plight as being caused by the factors just mentioned, as well as by the deportation of criminal aliens from the United States to Mexico without any coordination with local authorities. From a U.S. point of view, Mexico's institutional weakness and corruption are the source of its woes and the primary obstacle to more effective cooperation. Mexico's current crisis therefore presents an unprecedented opportunity for the two countries to work together to address shared challenges and responsibilities.

In recent years, Mexico has been highly receptive to binational cooperation with the United States, resulting in record numbers of extraditions and cross-border prosecutions. Such progress helped pave the way for targeted U.S. assistance since 2007 under the Mérida Initiative. The development of a clear framework for U.S.-Mexico cooperation is an achievement in itself. Working intensely and bilaterally, authorities from both countries have successfully identified shared priorities, strategies, and avenues for cooperation. For Mexico, direct U.S. financial assistance provides a significant boost to the roughly $4.3 billion already spent annually combating drug trafficking.[35]

Because the initial allotment of funds for the Mérida Initiative ended in fiscal year 2009–2010, the Obama administration worked with Mexican authorities to develop a longer-term, four-point framework for continued cooperation: more binational collaboration to combat DTOs, greater assistance to strengthen the judicial sector, more effective interdiction efforts through twenty-first-century border controls, and new social programs to revitalize Mexican communities affected by crime and violence.[36] In parallel, the U.S. government also plans to increase its efforts to address the central causes of Mexico's drug violence, to include new funding to reduce arms smuggling, money laundering, and illicit drug consumption in the United States. Also, reacting to public concerns, the United States has deployed massive manpower and funding to the U.S.-Mexico border to prevent undocumented immigration and stave off spillover violence.

## INTERAGENCY COOPERATION

International cooperation under the Mérida Initiative remains primarily coordinated by agencies in the U.S. Department of State.[37] Within the Department of State, the most prominent roles are played by the Bureau of Western Hemisphere Affairs (WHA), the Bureau of International Narcotics Affairs and Law Enforcement (INL), and the U.S. Agency for International Development (USAID).[38] The Department of Defense (DOD), particularly the U.S. Northern Command (NORTH-COM), has also begun to interact with its Mexican counterparts more regularly in recent years. High-level governmental coordination occurs through regular meetings of the Inter-Agency Policy Committee, organized by the National Security Council (NSC), and the Mérida Initiative Core Group. Midlevel and operational government task forces currently work together through several interagency and intra-agency coordination mechanisms, thanks in part to active leadership by the

U.S. Embassy in Mexico City. The United States has much to offer in formal governmental assistance and in academic and nongovernmental programs, such as the Commission on Accreditation for Law Enforcement Agencies (CALEA), the Open Society Justice Initiative, the American Bar Association (ABA), the National Center for State Courts (NCSC), and others.

The structures for coordination across U.S. and Mexican government initiatives are still in development, and ongoing challenges associated with the sudden increase in funding must be addressed to sustain and move beyond the current high-water mark in binational cooperation. Whether starting up or scaling up operations, many agencies and programs in both countries need additional resources, staff, and infrastructure. At the same time, many programs lack continuity beyond a specific budget cycle, have no coherent long-term strategy, and find it difficult to cooperate with complementary programs with which they compete for the same funding. With 90 percent of Mérida funding in 2011 channeled through INL, the emphasis will remain focused on so-called hard approaches, leaving other agencies—notably USAID—at a disadvantage. Even where adequate funding is present, political and bureaucratic obstacles—on the part of both the United States and Mexico—have delayed some programs and deliverables, contributing to frustration and criticism toward the Mérida Initiative. Meanwhile, because the Mérida Initiative is formally coordinated by the State Department, no high-level U.S. agency shares direct responsibility or leadership for dealing with the intermestic problems associated with transnational organized crime networks. Finally, many programs place too little emphasis on monitoring performance indicators and measuring effectiveness.[39] Left unaddressed, these problems may contribute to unnecessary inefficiencies, duplication of efforts, inconsistent metrics of success, and confusion and dissatisfaction among partners and stakeholders in Mexico.

## U.S. DEVELOPMENT ASSISTANCE TO MEXICO

Despite the major differences between Mexico and Colombia, U.S. efforts to support Mexico can draw some lessons from its efforts in Colombia. U.S. antidrug assistance through Plan Colombia greatly bolstered the capacity of the Colombian state to combat DTOs and make long-term gains in citizen security. Although Plan Colombia exhibited many flaws—including human rights violations and unresolved problems of violence and internal displacement—intense binational cooperation, intelligence sharing, and joint tactical operations provided a decisive advantage against both DTOs and insurgent threats. Military and law enforcement assistance was only part of the equation. Robust economic assistance, averaging $200 million a year over the past five years, has consolidated security gains in Colombia. Furthermore, this aid facilitated the transformation of Colombia's urban slums into resilient communities and helped decrease unemployment from 15 percent to 11 percent.

In contrast, current U.S. priorities in Mexico remain focused on the hard and tactical measures more relevant to rooting out Colombia's insurgents than to addressing the social, economic, and institutional factors that undermine public security in Mexico. The first three years of the Mérida Initiative consisted primarily of funds for military assistance, narcotics control, and law enforcement, and more than half of all funding was directed to aircraft, transportation units, and equipment. Meanwhile, even as the current binational strategy emphasizes judicial sector reform and building strong communities, only a trivial portion of U.S. aid to Mexico is slated for institutional strengthening and development assistance. As a result, Mexico ranks among the lowest U.S. priorities in Latin America, even though Mexico's forty million poor people outnumber the individual populations of all but two other countries in the region (Argentina and Brazil). As a necessary complement to hard law enforcement measures, the United States should begin directing its money and efforts to the kind of social, economic, and institutional development assistance that can help fund crime prevention programs, educational assistance, workforce development in struggling communities, and greater professionalism and effectiveness in the judicial sector.

## RETHINKING U.S. DRUG POLICY

Mexico's security crisis illustrates the limitations of current antidrug strategies and offers an opportunity to shift the paradigm to a more sensible approach. Over the past four decades, the war on drugs has lacked clear, consistent, or achievable objectives; has had little effect on aggregate demand; and has imposed an enormous social and economic cost.[40]

A state-driven, supply-side, and penalty-based approach has failed to curb market production, distribution, and consumption of drugs. The assumption that punishing suppliers and users can effectively combat a large market for illicit drugs has been proven utterly false. Rather, prohibition bestows enormous profits on traffickers, criminalizes otherwise law-abiding users and addicts, and imposes enormous costs on society.[41] Meanwhile, there has been no real effect on the availability of drugs or their consumption, and three-quarters of U.S. citizens believe that the war on drugs has failed.[42]

One flaw of current U.S.-Mexico strategy is the false presumption that international trafficking of drugs, guns, and cash can be effectively addressed through interdiction, particularly along the nearly two-thousand-mile U.S.-Mexico border. After a three-decade effort to beef up security, the border is more heavily fortified than at any point since the U.S.-Mexico war of 1846–48. The United States has deployed more than twenty thousand border patrol agents and built hundreds of miles of fencing equipped with high-tech surveillance equipment, all at an annual cost of tens of billions of dollars. Although this massive security buildup at the border has yielded the highest possible operational control, the damage to Mexico's drug cartels caused by border interdiction has been inconsequential.[43] Meanwhile, heightened interdiction at the border has had several unintended consequences, including added hassles and delays that obstruct billions of dollars in legitimate commerce each year, the expansion and increased sophistication of cross-border smuggling operations, and greater U.S. vulnerability to attacks and even infiltration by traffickers.[44] Further efforts to beef up the border through more patrolling and fencing will have diminishing returns, and will likely cause more economic harm than gains in security for the struggling communities of the border region.[45]

Given the limits of U.S. drug policy, more information and analysis are needed to weigh the costs and benefits of current efforts against alternative policy options. For example, one recent study suggests that legalizing marijuana would cause as much as $1 billion to $2 billion in losses for Mexican drug traffickers, because competition from legally registered producers would drive them out of the business. Because these DTOs would continue to smuggle other profitable illicit drugs, the main benefit of marijuana legalization would be to allow U.S. border security and law enforcement to focus their resources on other problems.[46] Of course, although support for this idea is growing, the potential hazards and limitations of drug legalization are substantial.[47] Legalization would almost certainly cause drug traffickers to move into other illicit activities to maintain profitability, and U.S. and Mexican authorities would therefore still need to develop better measures to combat kidnapping, robbery, extortion, and other forms of organized crime. Meanwhile, as with other controlled substances, like tobacco and alcohol, increased recreational drug use would likely result in widespread use and significant social harm in both countries, including traffic fatalities, fatal overdoses, addiction, and chronic health problems.

Any effort to legalize drugs would need to proceed with careful study, ample deliberation, and due caution. Yet, with or without legalization, authorities should work with greater urgency and focus to develop public health and law enforcement measures to prevent, treat, and reduce the harms associated with drug consumption.[48] In the end, treating drug consumption and organized crime as separate problems will make it possible to address both more effectively. To make this possible—and before other countries or even some U.S. states venture further down the road toward drug legalization—the U.S. federal government should move quickly to examine the current approach and chart a course toward a more effective drug policy.

# Recommendations for U.S. Policy

Mexico urgently needs to reduce the power of violent organized crime groups; a prolonged failure to do so has seriously impaired both Mexican governance and Mexican economic prospects. Mexico's security crisis increasingly threatens U.S. interests, as well as the security and prosperity of other countries in the region, particularly in Central America, given the rapidly rising homicide rates, geographically expanding patterns of violence, and growing effects of violent organized crime on society. Though far from being a failed state, Mexico's current trajectory is dire, and doing nothing will ensure that greater violence and instability continue. The danger of recent strategies is that they have greatly exacerbated extreme violence among DTOs for the near term, and even if successful in the long run will merely cause them to relocate to neighboring countries—such as Guatemala, Nicaragua, and Costa Rica—that are less prepared to respond to the challenge.

The United States can help overcome Mexico's security crisis and prevent future problems elsewhere in three ways. First, it should build on recent progress and successes by enhancing and consolidating the mechanisms for bilateral and multilateral security cooperation in Mexico and Central America. Second, it should focus more seriously on U.S. drug demand, firearms, and money laundering at home, and direct greater assistance for institutional and economic development in Mexico. Finally, it should begin working toward a more sensible drug policy that includes alternative approaches to reducing the harms caused by drugs.

# ENHANCING AND CONSOLIDATING COOPERATION

## STRENGTHEN U.S. INTERAGENCY COOPERATION AND LIAISON MECHANISMS

The executive branch should establish mechanisms to coordinate U.S. responses to Mexico's security crisis domestically and abroad, including a White House office (special assistant) to facilitate sustained, high-level attention to U.S.-Mexico security cooperation, coordinate interagency processes, and monitor developments and progress. At the state level, the federal government should support collaboration among the U.S.-Mexico border governors and border legislators. Along the border, the United States should dedicate greater staff and resources to binational border liaison mechanisms (BLMs), as well as multiagency task forces and international liaison units within U.S. law enforcement agencies.

## PREVENT SPILLOVER TO CENTRAL AMERICA AND THE CARIBBEAN

The U.S. and Mexican agencies cooperating through the Mérida Initiative should convene regularly to coordinate with agencies working within the Caribbean Community and Common Market (CARICOM), the Caribbean Basin Security Initiative (CBSI), and the Central America Regional Security Initiative (CARSI). Additional resources and new initiatives are also needed to develop fusion centers, joint operations, and training to strengthen Central American and Caribbean capabilities in response to organized crime.

## INSTITUTIONALIZE MULTILATERAL FRAMEWORKS FOR REGIONAL SECURITY COOPERATION

The U.S. government should strengthen the Security and Prosperity Partnership or launch a similar initiative, creating a permanent, multilateral council of nongovernmental, private-sector, and elected representatives. The council should meet regularly to assesses the region's challenges and opportunities and promote sustained cooperation on matters related to security, trade, and regional integration.

### DEVELOP EXPLICIT PERFORMANCE MEASURES
### FOR THE FIGHT AGAINST ORGANIZED CRIME

Across the board, U.S. agencies should establish explicit baseline indicators, performance measures, benchmarks, targets, and timelines for progress toward their strategic objectives of dismantling organized crime, strengthening rule of law, reducing illicit flows, and building stronger communities. Assessment efforts will require dedicated funding for both congressional oversight and nongovernmental monitoring efforts, and should go beyond typical measures (such as arrests, trainings, seizures, and program activities) to evaluate outcomes, such as reductions in DTO operational capability, violent crime and human rights violations, total consumption of illicit drugs, and gang participation rates. Recent judicial sector, crime victimization, and community surveys provide useful examples and baseline measures for future evaluation.

## STRENGTHENING U.S. DOMESTIC EFFORTS

### DISRUPT U.S. ORGANIZED CRIME NETWORKS
### LINKED TO MEXICAN SUPPLIERS

The United States should develop and implement a coordinated, nationwide interagency strategy for identifying, investigating, and disrupting the U.S. financial facilitators and retail distributors that support Mexican DTOs.

### DEVELOP BETTER CONTROLS TO PREVENT
### ILLEGAL U.S. FIREARMS EXPORTS TO MEXICO

The United States should develop stricter controls to prevent illegal exports of firearms to Mexico. This is best done through registration requirements for large-volume ammunition purchases and unassembled assault weapons kit imports, reporting requirements for multiple long-arms sales (similar to those for multiple handgun sales), increasing ATF capacity for the investigation of straw purchases and trafficking conspiracies, and enforcing the federal ban on imports of assault rifles not intended for sporting purposes. The federal government should also review the possible effects of a ban on assault weapons and .50 caliber sniper rifles, similar to provisions that have proved successful at the state level. Finally, federal policy on firearms tracing and gun crime data should also be examined with an eye toward removing obstacles to information sharing among law enforcement agencies and greater transparency in the public reporting of aggregate data on gun crimes.

### DEVELOP BETTER CONTROLS ON MONEY LAUNDERING AND DTO FINANCIAL OPERATIONS

The United States should provide more resources, training, and coordination mechanisms for state and local law enforcement agencies to better target, seize, and trace the proceeds of illicit drug sales. It should also aggressively enforce the Foreign Investment and National Security Act of 2007 to track the investments of Mexican drug traffickers in the United States. Additionally, it should establish joint operations to share data and intelligence on possible drug money laundering in Mexican and third-country financial institutions. Ultimately, the United States needs greater coordination and stronger initiatives from the U.S. Securities and Exchange Commission (SEC), Treasury Department, and Federal Deposit Insurance Corporation (FDIC) to conduct careful searches for financial patterns consistent with drug money laundering. If these institutions cannot do so, then the United States should create a new agency that will.

### REDUCE OBSTACLES TO ECONOMIC GROWTH AND LEGITIMATE COMMERCE AT THE BORDER

U.S. authorities should make greater efforts to encourage NAFTA trade by facilitating legitimate cross-border flows and stimulating economic opportunities for local communities on both sides of the border—particularly by aggressively expanding access, efficiency, and infrastructure for trusted traveler and exporter programs, such as the Secure Electronic Network for Travelers Rapid Inspection (SENTRI) and the Customs-Trade Partnership Against Terrorism (C-TPAT). Following examples along the U.S.-Canada border, both the United States and Mexico can also facilitate cross-border commerce, maximize efficiencies, and improve border security by permitting privately funded ports of entry—like the Buffalo–Fort Erie Peace Bridge—and developing shared facilities for north- and southbound inspections at border corridors.

### ASSESS CURRENT U.S. BORDER SECURITY
### AND LAW ENFORCEMENT INTERAGENCY
### COOPERATION AND INTEGRITY

The U.S. Congress should require the Department of Homeland Security to provide regular reports and greater detail—including information and statistics on activities, seizures, apprehensions, and aggregate costs—for border security initiatives and programs intended to facilitate interagency collaboration in combating drug trafficking, money laundering, and firearms trafficking in border communities, such as Operation Stonegarden. In addition, the U.S. Government Accountability Office should carefully assess the influences of transnational organized crime networks on U.S. border security and law enforcement, and ensure adequate resources to address possible vulnerabilities and breaches in integrity.

### PREVENT BLOWBACK FROM U.S. DEPORTATIONS
### OF CRIMINAL ALIENS

U.S. law enforcement, prison, and immigration authorities should work more closely with their foreign counterparts to prevent repatriated criminal aliens from becoming new recruits for DTOs in Mexico and Central America. Preventive strategies should include educational and rehabilitative programs for foreign nationals in U.S. prisons, such as working with Mexico's education ministry to provide the equivalent of a general education degree to Mexican criminal aliens during their incarceration in the United States. In addition, U.S. immigration authorities should be required to work with Mexican and Central American authorities to develop better bilateral protocols for managing the reentry of aliens to their home countries.

## REALLOCATING U.S. ASSISTANCE TO MEXICO

### INCREASE U.S. ECONOMIC AND EDUCATIONAL
### ASSISTANCE FOR MEXICO

In its provision of aid, the United States should put greater emphasis on soft economic and educational assistance in addition to hard security assistance. The U.S. Congress should fully fund the Obama administration's request for $66 million in economic and development assistance for FY2012—more than doubling the amount provided in FY2010. In determining longer-term aid targets, policymakers should consider Plan Colombia's success in promoting economic development; Colombia has one-third Mexico's population, but it receives three times the economic and development assistance. By increasing economic assistance, the United States can provide alternative opportunities for poor families and micro-entrepreneurs in communities vulnerable to violence. Emphasis should be placed on broadening and scaling up programs of youth education, recreational and gang intervention programs, drug treatment and prevention, workforce preparation and technical training, microfinance and microcredit lending, and regional economic development and job-creation centers. In addition, the Obama administration should bolster funding for international educational and professional exchanges, encouraging skills transference and sustained partnerships that build knowledge and opportunities in both Mexico and the United States.

### INCREASE U.S. ASSISTANCE FOR JUDICIAL REFORM IN MEXICO

The United States should greatly expand its efforts to assist Mexican judicial sector reform. In particular, it should broaden and enhance support for education, training, and exchange programs for judicial sector professionals; nongovernmental organizations that monitor judicial sector performance, advocate for due process, and promote human rights; and efforts to develop independent measures of judicial sector performance in Mexico. Greater emphasis should be placed especially on coordination and cross-fertilization among U.S.-funded programs in these areas, and on baseline and performance indicators to demonstrate progress in the short (one to three years) and intermediate (three to five years) terms.

## SHIFTING U.S. DRUG POLICY

### REEVALUATE U.S. DRUG POLICY

The U.S. Congress should commission an independent advisory group to examine the fiscal and social effects of drug legalization as well as other alternative approaches to the war on drugs. The commission should be provided enough funding—at least $2 million—to provide a comprehensive review of existing policies and develop realistic, clearly defined, and achievable policy recommendations for reducing the harms caused by drug consumption and abuse.

### SHIFT U.S. COUNTER-DRUG PRIORITIES TO FOCUS ON MAJOR SOURCES OF ILLICIT INCOME

To allow policy experimentation, the federal government should permit states to legalize the production, sale, taxation, and consumption of marijuana. While testing this policy shift, authorities should redirect scarce law enforcement resources to focus on the more damaging and socially unacceptable drugs (such as heroin, cocaine, and methamphetamine) from which Mexican DTOs derive more than 70 percent of their drug proceeds.

### LEAD INTERNATIONAL EFFORTS ON DRUG POLICY REFORM

The United States should lead the dialogue on the future of international drug policy by collaborating directly with other countries in the Americas to develop alternative policy approaches to reduce the harm caused by drugs. Specifically, the United States and Mexico should work together in promoting the Inter-American Drug Abuse Control Commission's New Hemispheric Drug Strategy, with an emphasis on protections for basic human rights, evidence-based drug policy, and a public health approach to drug abuse.

## FINAL OBSERVATIONS

The opportunity for effective U.S.-Mexico cooperation to address these shared concerns has grown, thanks to the resolve of Mexican leaders to embrace the fight against transnational organized crime. The United States clearly has a vested interest in helping Mexico improve its governance, national security, economic productivity, and quality of life, which are integral to making Mexico a better neighbor and trade partner in the longer term. Mexico is also eager to continue working toward these ends, and it has embraced unprecedented levels of collaboration.

Over the next five years, the best-case scenario will bring a turning point in which authorities gain the upper hand against organized crime, violence dies down to pre-2006 levels, and illicit drug flows diminish dramatically. This would require continued progress in disrupting organized crime groups, with the reduction in drug-related violence the primary metric of policy success. For now, at least, the nightmare scenarios of government collapse, widespread political insurgency, or sudden military takeover are as unlikely in Mexico as they are in Brazil and Colombia, which have even higher levels of violence. Still, without progress on the noted recommendations, Mexico's drug war will drag onward and downward indefinitely, with greater and more geographically dispersed violence, more direct political influences by organized crime, rising instability and fear, growing human and capital flight, and increasing spillover effects to neighboring countries, including the United States.

Challenges and setbacks are inevitable, and building greater trust and cooperation will require sustained efforts. Events in late 2010 and early 2011, such as WikiLeaks' disclosure of persistent skepticism within the U.S. embassy in Mexico City of Calderón's government and military performance, and the death of a U.S. immigration and customs agent at the hands of drug traffickers, led to an unexpected nadir in U.S.-Mexico relations. The surprise Obama-Calderón summit of March 2011 reflects both countries' desire to move past short-term diplomatic disruptions. The United States can help shift the balance in Mexico's battle against organized crime and prevent the further spread of violence within Mexico and to its neighbors. This will require a serious commitment to U.S. responsibilities at home, long-term investments to make Mexico a more secure and prosperous neighbor, greater multilateral cooperation throughout the region, and a more sensible policy for managing the harms associated with drugs.

# Endnotes

1. A widely cited 2008 worst-case assessment by the U.S. Joint Forces Command (US-JFCOM) made the questionable assertion that Mexico was one of two countries—along with Pakistan—that could suffer a sudden collapse into a failed state in the near future. Specifically, the report asserted that "in terms of worst-case scenarios for the Joint Force and indeed the world, two large and important states bear consideration for a rapid and sudden collapse: Pakistan and Mexico." Russell D. Howard and Reid L. Sawyer, *Terrorism and Counterterrorism: Understanding the New Security Environment, Readings & Interpretations*, rev. and updated ed. (Guilford, CT: McGraw-Hill/Dushkin, 2004).

2. The calculation of total homicides is based on rates reported by the United Nations Office on Drugs and Crime (UNODC) and CIA World Factbook population estimates for 2007, 2008, 2009, and 2010. Jorge Ramos, "Gobierno revela mapa de guerra entre cárteles," *El Universal*, August 28, 2010; "28 mil 353 ejecutados en el sexenio. Radiografía del crimen organizado," *Milenio*, August 28, 2010; "Mexico: Safer than Canada," *Economist*, August 27, 2010.

3. The U.S. government defines *spillover violence* as DTO attacks targeting U.S. assets, but excludes DTO versus DTO violence on U.S. territory or elsewhere.

4. Although the exact proportion of U.S. firearms that are responsible for Mexico's violence is debated, that these number in the tens of thousands is not in question. Eric Olson, Andrew Selee, and David A. Shirk, *Shared Responsibility: U.S.-Mexico Policy Options for Combating Organized Crime* (Washington, DC: Mexico Institute, Woodrow Wilson International Center for Scholars/San Diego, CA: Trans-Border Institute, 2010).

5. Nacha Cattan, "Mexican Drug Traffickers Set Up New Cells in Central America," *Christian Science Monitor*, December 30, 2010.

6. The Government Accountability Office reports that $1.32 billion (84 percent) of Mérida Initiative funding was slated for Mexico, and $258 million (16 percent) for Central America. *Mérida Initiative: The United States Has Provided Counternarcotics and Anticrime Support but Needs Better Performance Measures* (Washington, DC: U.S. Printing Office, 2010), p. 4.

7. Presentation by sociologist Marcelo Bergman at the Woodrow Wilson International Center for Scholars in April 2010. See also Jose Brambila Macias, *Modeling the Informal Economy in Mexico. A Structural Equation Approach*, Munich, 2008, http://mpra.ub.uni-muenchen.de/8504/.

8. Drug trafficking creates a wide range of relatively flexible job opportunities at different levels of specialization: pilots, drivers, and logistics experts; lookouts, enforcers, and professional hit men; accountants and financial experts; and top-level cartel executives in the drug trade. The U.S. government estimates total profits from these activities to be between $19 billion and $39 billion, whereas the Mexican government has long

estimated $11 billion to $12 billion annually. The figures range between 1 percent and 3 percent of Mexico's $1.4 trillion GDP. A recent Rand study provides the most careful estimate available to date, placing annual Mexican drug gross revenues from the United States, not including other revenues, at around $6 billion to $7 billion, or 0.5 percent of GDP. Howard Campbell, *Drug War Zone* (Austin: University of Texas Press, 2009); Beau Kilmer, Jonathan P. Caulkins, Brittany M. Bond, and Peter H. Reuter, *Reducing Drug Trafficking Revenues and Violence in Mexico: Would Legalizing Marijuana in California Help?* (occasional paper, Rand Corporation, Santa Monica, CA, 2010).

9. The calculation of forty-five thousand total homicides is based on official rates published by the United Nations Office on Drugs and Crime (UNODC) and CIA World Factbook population estimates for 2007, 2008, and 2009. See also David A. Shirk, *Drug Violence in Mexico: Data and Analysis from 2001–2009* (San Diego: Trans-Border Institute, 2010).

10. In 2010 alone, fourteen of the country's roughly 2,450 mayors were assassinated. Viridiana Ríos and David A. Shirk, *Drug Violence in Mexico: Data and Analysis through 2010* (San Diego, CA: Trans-Border Institute, 2011); Redacción, "EU: el *narco* asesinó a 61 enlaces de DEA y FBI," *Público* 14, no. 4808 (December 4, 2010), p. 28.

11. "Periodistas demandan justicia y abatir violencia," *El Universal*, July 9, 2010; "Urge frenar ataques a medios: CIDH y SIP," *El Universal*, August 28, 2010.

12. María Celia Toro, *Mexico's "War" on Drugs: Causes and Consequences* (Boulder, CO: Lynne Rienner, 1995).

13. The most comprehensive analysis of drug trafficking in Mexico has been conducted by Luis Astorga. Luis Alejandro Astorga Almanza, *Seguridad, traficantes y militares: el poder y la sombra* (Mexico City: Tusquets, 2007), *El siglo de las drogas: el narcotráfico, del Porfiriato al nuevo milenio* (Mexico City: Plaza y Janís, 2005), *Drogas sin fronteras* (Mexico City: Grijalbo, 2003), "Traficantes de drogas, políticos y policías en el siglo XX mexicano," in *Vicios públicos, virtudes privadas: La corrupción en México*, edited by C. Lomnitz (Mexico City: CIESAS, 2000). See also Carlos Antonio Flores Pérez, "Organized Crime and Official Corruption in Mexico," in *Police and Public Security in Mexico*, Robert A. Donnelly and David A. Shirk, eds. (San Diego: Trans-Border Institute, 2009).

14. Luis Alejandro Astorga Almanza and David A. Shirk, "Drug Trafficking Organizations and Counter-Drug Strategies in the U.S.-Mexican Context," in Eric L. Olson, David A. Shirk, and Andrew D. Selee, eds., *Shared Responsibility: U.S.-Mexico Policy Options for Confronting Organized Crime* (Washington, DC: Mexico Institute, Woodrow Wilson International Center for Scholars/San Diego, CA: Trans-Border Institute, 2010); Richard Snyder and Angelica Duran-Martinez, "Does Illegality Breed Violence? Drug Trafficking and State-Sponsored Protection Rackets," *Crime, Law, and Social Change* 52, no. 3 (2009), pp. 253–73.

15. The first major deployments began at the outset of the Calderón administration in December 2006 with the introduction of 6,700 troops to Michoacán, then Mexico's most violent state. As the violence spread, troop deployments were expanded to other areas in Baja California, Guerrero, Nuevo León, Sinaloa, Tamaulipas, and Veracruz. Since 2008, Mexico's major deployments have been concentrated in the state of Chihuahua, which presently accounts for the largest proportion of Mexico's drug violence.

16. Some states, such as Michoacán and Tamaulipas, saw significant reductions in drug-related violence after federal forces were deployed there in 2007, but both experienced sharp increases in 2010. Other states, like Chihuahua, Guerrero, and Nuevo León, suffered continued or increased violence after the arrival of the military.

17. From 2006 to 2010, more than 4,200 formal complaints were issued to Mexico's human rights ombudsman, yet according to the Mexican military only around 2

percent of these resulted in formal action. Accusations of misconduct include torture, cruel and degrading treatment, arbitrary detention, dangerous incarceration conditions, and falsification of evidence in human rights investigations. For more on the role of the military, see Roderick Camp, "Armed Forces and Drugs: Public Perceptions and Institutional Challenges" (occasional paper, Mexico Institute, Woodrow Wilson International Center for Scholars, Washington, DC, 2010).

18. George Grayson, "Los Zetas: the Ruthless Army Spawned by a Mexican Drug Cartel" (bulletin, Foreign Policy Research Institute, Washington, DC, 2008).

19. Public opinion polls generally support the government's efforts to combat DTOs, but also tend to see the government as losing the fight. "Economía, gobierno y política," *Consulta Mitofsky,* January 2010. Recent blows against the La Familia Michoacana organization in Michoacán resulted in public demonstrations of support for the traffickers. William Finnegan, "Silver or Lead," *New Yorker,* May 31, 2010; Elly Castillo, "Muestran apoyo a *La Familia* en Apatzingán," *El Universal,* December 12, 2010.

20. Nathan Pino and Michael D. Wiatrowski, *Democratic Policing in Transitional and Developing Countries* (Burlington, VT: Ashgate, 2006); David H. Bayley, *Democratizing the Police Abroad: What to Do and How to Do It* (Washington, DC: U.S. Department of Justice, 2001); Joseph S. Tulchin and Meg Ruthenburg, *Toward a Society under Law: Citizens and Their Police in Latin America* (Washington, DC: Woodrow Wilson Center Press/Baltimore, MD: Johns Hopkins University Press, 2006).

21. Recent police surveys in Guadalajara and Ciudad Juárez found that 80 percent of local police earn less than $800 per month; the vast majority reported working more than fifty hours a week with no overtime pay and erratic shifts that seriously diminish job performance. Due to weak civil service protections, police promotions are based not on merit but on personal connections. Also, frequent administrative changes result in a constant reshuffling of personnel that undermines effective program building, reduces corps morale, and erodes institutional knowledge. María Eugenia Suárez de Garay, Marcos Pablo Moloeznik, and David A. Shirk, *Justiciabarómetro: Estudio de la policía municipal preventiva de la Zona Metropolitana de Guadalajara* (Guadalajara: Universidad de Guadalajara, 2010); María Eugenia Suárez de Garay, Marcos Pablo Moloeznik, and David A. Shirk, *Justiciabarómetro: Estudio de la policía municipal preventiva de Ciudad Juárez* (forthcoming).

22. Centralizing the functions of police at the state level could help bring greater efficiency, homogeneity, and resource capacity to Mexican law enforcement. However, neither the *federales* nor the state police are less vulnerable to corruption than local police, and organized crime would likely exploit the very same advantages reformers hope to achieve: unity of command, organizational efficiency, and economies of scale. For this reason, Mexican authorities would do well to take a more targeted approach, subsuming local law enforcement only as a last resort in extremely troubled municipalities.

23. Instituto Ciudadano de Estudios Sobre la Inseguridad (ICESI), www.icesi.org.mx.

24. Guillermo Zepeda Lecuona, *Crimen sin castigo: Procuración de justicia penal y ministerio público en México* (Mexico City: Centro de Investigación Para el Desarrollo, A.C. Fondo de Cultura Económica, 2004).

25. Although the probability of being arrested, investigated, and prosecuted for a crime is extremely low, as many as 85 percent of crime suspects arrested are found guilty, and at least half of all prisoners are convicted for property crimes valued at less than $20. Ricardo Hernández Forcada and María Elena Lugo Garfias, *Algunas notas sobre la tortura en México* (Mexico City: Comisión Nacional de los Derechos Humanos, 2004), p. 139; International Rehabilitation Council for Torture Victims (IRCT), *Country Assessment Report: Mexico* (Copenhagen: International Rehabilitation Council for Torture Victims, 2006), p. 8; Elena Azaola and Marcelo Bergman, "The Mexican Prison

System," in *Reforming the Administation of Justice in Mexico*, Wayne A. Cornelius and David A. Shirk, eds. (Notre Dame, IN: Notre Dame Press/La Jolla, CA: Center for U.S.-Mexican Studies, 2007).

26. Elena Azaola and Marcelo Bergman, *Delincuencia, marginalidad y desempeño institucional: Resultados de la tercera encuesta a población en reclusión en el Distrito Federal y el Estado de México* (Mexico City: Centro de Investigación y Docencia Económicas, 2009).

27. These judicial sector reforms significantly alter the functioning of Mexico's variant of the inquisitorial criminal justice system by introducing elements (such as oral adversarial trials, alternative sentencing, and alternative dispute resolution mechanisms) found in adversarial systems, such as that of the United States. Matthew C. Ingram and David A. Shirk, *Judicial Reform in Mexico: Toward a New Criminal Justice System* (San Diego, CA: Trans-Border Institute, 2010).

28. These drugs included marijuana, cocaine, crack cocaine, heroin, hallucinogens, inhalants, and nonmedical use of prescription psychotherapeutic drugs. Marijuana was the most commonly used illicit drug, with 16.7 million past-month users accounting for more than 76 percent of current drug use. 2.8 million of all users received treatment for illicit drug use and/or other substance abuse. *Results from the 2009 National Survey on Drug Use and Health: National Findings* (Rockville, MD: Substance Abuse and Mental Health Services Administration, Office of Applied Studies, September 2010).

29. Black markets can make goods either cheaper or more expensive. When a good is legally available but overpriced, as with pirated music or cigarettes in Canada, black market prices tend to be lower than the free market. However, when a good is illegal and, especially, controlled by a small group or cartel, as with illicit drugs, its price tends to become inflated relative to what it might be on the free market. Whereas U.S. official estimates suggest that marijuana represents 60 percent of drug profits, a recent Rand study places total Mexican DTO drug gross revenues from the United States at around $6 billion to $7 billion, with up to one-quarter coming from marijuana. Kilmer et al., *Reducing Drug Trafficking Revenues and Violence in Mexico*.

30. Michael Smith, "Banks Financing Mexico Gangs Admitted in Wells Fargo Deal," *Bloomberg News*, June 29, 2010, http://www.bloomberg.com/news/2010-06-29/banks-financing-mexico-s-drug-cartels-admitted-in-wells-fargo-s-u-s-deal.html.

31. Estimates for the number of gun shops along the border vary widely. In January 2008, Mexican ambassador Arturo Sarukhán indicated that "between Texas and Arizona alone, you've got 12,000 gun shops along that border with Mexico" (Alfredo Corchado and Tim Connolly, "U.S. Seeks Unity Against Drug Trade," *Dallas Morning News*, January 16, 2008). More recent estimates place the figure around 6,700, approximately three gun dealers for every mile along the border. Richard A. Serrano, "Guns from U.S. equip drug cartels," *Los Angeles Times*, August 10, 2008. Estimates for the total number of gun dealers in the United States also vary, but by all accounts they have declined dramatically over the past decade—from 245,000 to 54,000—thanks to tighter regulations. Alexandra Marks, "Why Gun Dealers Have Dwindled," *Christian Science Monitor*, March 14, 2006. See also Jon S. Vernick, Daniel W. Webster, Maria T. Bulzacchelli, and Julie Samia Mair, "Regulation of Firearm Dealers in the United States: An Analysis of State Law and Opportunities for Improvement," *Journal of Law, Medicine, and Ethics* 34, no. 4 (2006), pp. 765–75.

32. According to the 2004 national firearms survey, there are an estimated 218 million privately owned firearms in the United States. L. Hepburn, M. Miller, D. Azrael, D. Hemenway, "The US gun stock: results from the 2004 national firearms survey," *Injury Prevention*, 2007. However, only one in four U.S. citizens (26 percent) and two in five households (38 percent) actually owned a firearm. This means that the vast majority of

firearms are owned by a small percentage of the population: nearly half (48 percent) of all individual gun owners own four or more weapons, and only one-fifth (20 percent) own 65 percent of all guns.

33. President Obama has voiced support for the Inter-American Convention Against the Illicit Manufacturing of and Trafficking in Firearms, Ammunition, Explosives, and Other Related Materials, promulgated by the Organization of American States and better known by its Spanish acronym (CIFTA). CIFTA was initially signed by President Bill Clinton in 1997 but has yet to be submitted for the Senate's advice and consent on ratification.

34. For example, California has had significant success in reducing the accessibility of .50 caliber sniper rifles by imposing tough restrictions supported by U.S. law enforcement agencies. Moreover, comparative analysis demonstrates a strong correlation between state and local laws and illegal interstate trafficking. Mayors Against Illegal Guns, "Trace the Guns: The Link between Gun Laws and Interstate Gun Trafficking," 2010.

35. Query to Ambassador Arturo Sarukhán at a presentation to the Mexico Institute of the Woodrow Wilson Center in 2010.

36. Clare Ribando Seelke and Kristin M. Finklea, "U.S.-Mexican Security Cooperation: the Mérida Initiative and Beyond," CRS Report R41349 (Washington, DC: Congressional Research Service, 2010).

37. Current coordination mechanisms have no role for the Ministry of the Interior (*Gobernación*), the federal judiciary, or the Mexican state executive and judicial branches (for example, the National Council of State Courts, CONATRIB).

38. Given concerns about preventing human rights violations, it is notable that the Bureau of Democracy, Human Rights, and Labor (DRL), under the undersecretary for democracy and global affairs, does not appear to play a prominent role under Mérida.

39. For example, the amount of drugs seized says nothing about the effect on aggregate supply and demand. Likewise, the number of judicial system operatives trained does not account for the quality or influence of that training. U.S. Government Accountability Office, "Mérida Initiative: The United States Has Provided Counternarcotics and Anticrime Support but Needs Better Performance Measures," GAO-10-837 (Washington, DC: U.S. Government Accountability Office, 2010).

40. Peter Reuter points out that policy is generally a far weaker influence on demand for drugs than cultural norms, and in any event prevention programs do not have significant near-term effects on overall market demand. "How Can Domestic U.S. Drug Policy Help Mexico?" in Olson, Shirk, and Selee, eds., *Shared Responsibility: U.S.-Mexico Policy Options for Confronting Organized Crime*, pp. 121–40.

41. At a keynote address presented at the Fifth International Conference on Drug Policy Reform in Washington, DC, on November 16, 1991, Nobel Prize–winning economist Milton Friedman argued, "The war on drugs is a failure because it is a socialist enterprise. . . . The U.S. government enforces a drug cartel. The major beneficiaries from drug prohibition are the drug lords, who can maintain a cartel that they would be unable to maintain without current government policy." Arnold S. Trebach and Kevin B. Zeese, eds., *Friedman & Szasz on Liberty and Drugs* (Washington, DC: Drug Policy Foundation, 1992).

42. Peter Hakim, *Rethinking U.S. Drug Policy* (Washington, DC: Inter-American Dialogue/Beckley Foundation, 2011).

43. In 2009, U.S. authorities seized about 17,000 kilos of cocaine, or about $273 million at wholesale prices (roughly $16,000 per kilo), at the southwest border. However, authorities spent most of their time and manpower seizing the nearly 1.5 million kilos of marijuana that, in bulk terms (total poundage), represented 98 percent of all illicit drugs seized at the border. According to the best available estimates, these seizures

represented a small fraction, no more than 9 percent of the $6 billion to $7 billion in total proceeds that Mexican DTOs derive from the United States each year.

44. The number of Border Patrol agents alone increased from 2,900 in 1980 to 9,000 in 2000 to more than 20,000 by 2010. This has squeezed mom-and-pop smuggling operations out of the business, allowing more dangerous and powerful DTOs to take over. As a result, the Border Patrol has experienced more violent attacks (including fatalities) and hundreds of cases of corruption in its ranks since 2003. Ralph Vartabedian, Richard A. Serrano, and Richard Marosi, "The Long Crooked Line: Rise in Bribery Tests Integrity of U.S. Border," *Los Angeles Times*, October 23, 2006; Pauline Arrillaga, "Feds Struggle with Border Patrol Corruption," Associated Press, September 22, 2006; Randal C. Archibold and Andrew Becker, "Border Agents, Lured by the Other Side," *New York Times*, May 27, 2008.

45. The U.S. economy loses $3.74 billion of cross-border economic activity and more than thirty-three thousand jobs each year at the San Diego-Tijuana corridor alone, the entry point for 12 percent of overall U.S.-Mexico trade. *Economic Impacts of Wait Times at the San Diego-Baja California Border* (San Diego: San Diego Association Of Governments/California Department of Transportation, January 19, 2006), http://www.sandag.org/programs/borders/binational/projects/2006_border_wait_impacts_report.pdf. See also Hercules E. Haralambides and Maria P. Londono-Kent, "Supply Chain Bottlenecks: Border Crossing Inefficiencies between Mexico and the United States," *International Journal of Transport Economics* 31, no. 2 (June 2004), pp. 171–83.

46. In 2009, marijuana violations accounted for 6 percent of all domestic arrests within the United States, and more than half of all drug-related arrests. National Drug Intelligence Center, *2010 National Drug Threat Assessment*, table 1, "Drug Seizures Along the Southwest and Northern Borders, in Kilograms, 2005–2009" (Washington, DC: U.S. Department of Justice); Kilmer et al., *Reducing Drug Trafficking Revenues*; FBI Uniform Crime Statistics for 2009, http://www2.fbi.gov/ucr.

47. The General Social Survey (GSS) conducted biannually since 1972 has demonstrated an increase in support for marijuana legalization beginning in the 1990s, and recent 2010 polls suggest that such support is at an all-time high. Indeed, 46 percent of California voters (nearly 3.3 million people) favored legalization in a November 2010 ballot initiative. In Mexico, an April 2009 BGC-Ulises Beltrán poll suggested that support for legalization was slightly higher than in the United States at that time, with 40 percent supporting the legalization of marijuana. Mexicans showed much less support for legalization of other drugs, such as cocaine (17 percent), crack cocaine (14 percent), ecstasy (13 percent), methamphetamines (12 percent), and heroin (11 percent).The same poll reported that more than two-thirds of respondents perceived drug consumption to be a national problem in Mexico, rather than a regional problem. Forty-six percent supported giving addicts legal access to drugs during rehabilitation, and 49 percent opposed the option. Ulises Beltrán, "Rechazan Legalizar Drogas," *Excélsior*, 2009.

48. "Drugs and Democracy: Toward a Paradigm Shift," Latin American Commission on Drugs and Democracy, 2009, http://www.drogasedemocracia.org/Arquivos/declaracao_ingles_site.pdf.

# About the Author

David A. Shirk is the director of the Trans-Border Institute and associate professor of political science at the University of San Diego. He conducts research on Mexican politics, U.S.-Mexico relations, and law enforcement and security along the U.S.-Mexico border. Dr. Shirk received his PhD in political science at the University of California, San Diego, and was a fellow at the Center for U.S.-Mexican Studies from 1998 to 1999 and from 2001 to 2003. In 2009–2010, Dr. Shirk was a fellow at the Woodrow Wilson Center for International Scholars in Washington, DC. He is currently the principal investigator for the Justice in Mexico project (www.justiceinmexico.org), a binational research initiative on criminal justice and the rule of law in Mexico. Recent publications by Dr. Shirk include *Shared Responsibility: U.S.-Mexico Policy Options for Confronting Organized Crime*; *Justiciabarómetro: Estudio de la policía municipal preventiva de la Zona Metropolitana de Guadalajara*; *Judicial Reform in Mexico*; *Drug Violence in Mexico*; *Justiciabarómetro: Resultados de la encuesta a la policía municipal preventiva de la Zona Metropolitana de Guadalajara*; *Police and Public Security in Mexico*; *Contemporary Mexican Politics*; *Reforming the Administration of Justice in Mexico*; *Evaluating Accountability and Transparency in Mexico: National, Local, and Comparative Perspectives*; and *Mexico's New Politics: The PAN and Democratic Change*.

# Advisory Committee for
## *The Drug War in Mexico*

This report reflects the judgments and recommendations of the author(s). It does not necessarily represent the views of members of the advisory committee, whose involvement in no way should be interpreted as an endorsement of the report by either themselves or the organizations with which they are affiliated.

# Center for Preventive Action
# Advisory Committee

# Mission Statement of the Center for Preventive Action

The Center for Preventive Action (CPA) seeks to help prevent, defuse, or resolve deadly conflicts around the world and to expand the body of knowledge on conflict prevention. It does so by creating a forum in which representatives of governments, international organizations, nongovernmental organizations, corporations, and civil society can gather to develop operational and timely strategies for promoting peace in specific conflict situations. The center focuses on conflicts in countries or regions that affect U.S. interests, but may be otherwise overlooked; where prevention appears possible; and when the resources of the Council on Foreign Relations can make a difference. The center does this by

- Issuing Council Special Reports to evaluate and respond rapidly to developing conflict situations and formulate timely, concrete policy recommendations that the U.S. government, international community, and local actors can use to limit the potential for deadly violence.

- Engaging the U.S. government and news media in conflict prevention efforts. CPA staff members meet with administration officials and members of Congress to brief on CPA's findings and recommendations; facilitate contacts between U.S. officials and important local and external actors; and raise awareness among journalists of potential flashpoints around the globe.

- Building networks with international organizations and institutions to complement and leverage the Council's established influence in the U.S. policy arena and increase the impact of CPA's recommendations.

- Providing a source of expertise on conflict prevention to include research, case studies, and lessons learned from past conflicts that policymakers and private citizens can use to prevent or mitigate future deadly conflicts.

# Council Special Reports

*Published by the Council on Foreign Relations*

.

*UN Security Council Enlargement and U.S. Interests*
Kara C. McDonald and Stewart M. Patrick; CSR No. 59, December 2010
An International Institutions and Global Governance Program Report

*Congress and National Security*
Kay King; CSR No. 58, November 2010

*Toward Deeper Reductions in U.S. and Russian Nuclear Weapons*
Micah Zenko; CSR No. 57, November 2010
A Center for Preventive Action Report

*Internet Governance in an Age of Cyber Insecurity*
Robert K. Knake; CSR 56, September 2010
An International Institutions and Global Governance Program Report

*From Rome to Kampala: The U.S. Approach to the 2010 International Criminal Court Review Conference*
Vijay Padmanabhan; CSR No. 55, April 2010

*Strengthening the Nuclear Nonproliferation Regime*
Paul Lettow; CSR No. 54, April 2010
An International Institutions and Global Governance Program Report

*The Russian Economic Crisis*
Jeffrey Mankoff; CSR No. 53, April 2010

*Somalia: A New Approach*
Bronwyn E. Bruton; CSR No. 52, March 2010
A Center for Preventive Action Report

*The Future of NATO*
James M. Goldgeier; CSR No. 51, February 2010
An International Institutions and Global Governance Program Report

*The United States in the New Asia*
Evan A. Feigenbaum and Robert A. Manning; CSR No. 50, November 2009
An International Institutions and Global Governance Program Report

*Avoiding Transfers to Torture*
Ashley S. Deeks; CSR No. 35, June 2008

*Global FDI Policy: Correcting a Protectionist Drift*
David M. Marchick and Matthew J. Slaughter; CSR No. 34, June 2008
A Maurice R. Greenberg Center for Geoeconomic Studies Report

*Dealing with Damascus: Seeking a Greater Return on U.S.-Syria Relations*
Mona Yacoubian and Scott Lasensky; CSR No. 33, June 2008
A Center for Preventive Action Report

*Climate Change and National Security: An Agenda for Action*
Joshua W. Busby; CSR No. 32, November 2007
A Maurice R. Greenberg Center for Geoeconomic Studies Report

*Planning for Post-Mugabe Zimbabwe*
Michelle D. Gavin; CSR No. 31, October 2007
A Center for Preventive Action Report

*The Case for Wage Insurance*
Robert J. LaLonde; CSR No. 30, September 2007
A Maurice R. Greenberg Center for Geoeconomic Studies Report

*Reform of the International Monetary Fund*
Peter B. Kenen; CSR No. 29, May 2007
A Maurice R. Greenberg Center for Geoeconomic Studies Report

*Nuclear Energy: Balancing Benefits and Risks*
Charles D. Ferguson; CSR No. 28, April 2007

*Nigeria: Elections and Continuing Challenges*
Robert I. Rotberg; CSR No. 27, April 2007
A Center for Preventive Action Report

*The Economic Logic of Illegal Immigration*
Gordon H. Hanson; CSR No. 26, April 2007
A Maurice R. Greenberg Center for Geoeconomic Studies Report

*The United States and the WTO Dispute Settlement System*
Robert Z. Lawrence; CSR No. 25, March 2007
A Maurice R. Greenberg Center for Geoeconomic Studies Report

*Bolivia on the Brink*
Eduardo A. Gamarra; CSR No. 24, February 2007
A Center for Preventive Action Report

*After the Surge: The Case for U.S. Military Disengagement from Iraq*
Steven N. Simon; CSR No. 23, February 2007

*Darfur and Beyond: What Is Needed to Prevent Mass Atrocities*
Lee Feinstein; CSR No. 22, January 2007

*Avoiding Conflict in the Horn of Africa: U.S. Policy Toward Ethiopia and Eritrea*
Terrence Lyons; CSR No. 21, December 2006
A Center for Preventive Action Report

*Living with Hugo: U.S. Policy Toward Hugo Chávez's Venezuela*
Richard Lapper; CSR No. 20, November 2006
A Center for Preventive Action Report

*Reforming U.S. Patent Policy: Getting the Incentives Right*
Keith E. Maskus; CSR No. 19, November 2006
A Maurice R. Greenberg Center for Geoeconomic Studies Report

*Foreign Investment and National Security: Getting the Balance Right*
Alan P. Larson and David M. Marchick; CSR No. 18, July 2006
A Maurice R. Greenberg Center for Geoeconomic Studies Report

*Challenges for a Postelection Mexico: Issues for U.S. Policy*
Pamela K. Starr; CSR No. 17, June 2006 (Web-only release) and November 2006

*U.S.-India Nuclear Cooperation: A Strategy for Moving Forward*
Michael A. Levi and Charles D. Ferguson; CSR No. 16, June 2006

*Generating Momentum for a New Era in U.S.-Turkey Relations*
Steven A. Cook and Elizabeth Sherwood-Randall; CSR No. 15, June 2006

*Peace in Papua: Widening a Window of Opportunity*
Blair A. King; CSR No. 14, March 2006
A Center for Preventive Action Report

*Neglected Defense: Mobilizing the Private Sector to Support Homeland Security*
Stephen E. Flynn and Daniel B. Prieto; CSR No. 13, March 2006

*Afghanistan's Uncertain Transition From Turmoil to Normalcy*
Barnett R. Rubin; CSR No. 12, March 2006
A Center for Preventive Action Report

*Preventing Catastrophic Nuclear Terrorism*
Charles D. Ferguson; CSR No. 11, March 2006

*Getting Serious About the Twin Deficits*
Menzie D. Chinn; CSR No. 10, September 2005
A Maurice R. Greenberg Center for Geoeconomic Studies Report

*Both Sides of the Aisle: A Call for Bipartisan Foreign Policy*
Nancy E. Roman; CSR No. 9, September 2005

*Forgotten Intervention? What the United States Needs to Do in the Western Balkans*
Amelia Branczik and William L. Nash; CSR No. 8, June 2005
A Center for Preventive Action Report

*A New Beginning: Strategies for a More Fruitful Dialogue with the Muslim World*
Craig Charney and Nicole Yakatan; CSR No. 7, May 2005

*Power-Sharing in Iraq*
David L. Phillips; CSR No. 6, April 2005
A Center for Preventive Action Report

*Giving Meaning to "Never Again": Seeking an Effective Response to the Crisis
in Darfur and Beyond*
Cheryl O. Igiri and Princeton N. Lyman; CSR No. 5, September 2004

*Freedom, Prosperity, and Security: The G8 Partnership with Africa: Sea Island 2004 and Beyond*
J. Brian Atwood, Robert S. Browne, and Princeton N. Lyman; CSR No. 4, May 2004

*Addressing the HIV/AIDS Pandemic: A U.S. Global AIDS Strategy for the Long Term*
Daniel M. Fox and Princeton N. Lyman; CSR No. 3, May 2004
Cosponsored with the Milbank Memorial Fund

*Challenges for a Post-Election Philippines*
Catharin E. Dalpino; CSR No. 2, May 2004
A Center for Preventive Action Report

*Stability, Security, and Sovereignty in the Republic of Georgia*
David L. Phillips; CSR No. 1, January 2004
A Center for Preventive Action Report

To purchase a printed copy, call the Brookings Institution Press: 800.537.5487.
*Note:* Council Special Reports are available for download from CFR's website, www.cfr.org.
For more information, email publications@cfr.org.